Native
American
Peoples

MOHAWK

Sierra Adare

Gareth Stevens
Publishing

Please visit our web site at: www.garethstevens.com
For a free color catalog describing Gareth Stevens Publishing's list of high-quality books,
call 1-800-542-2595 (USA) or 1-800-387-3178 (Canada).
Gareth Stevens Publishing's fax: 1-877-542-2596

Library of Congress Cataloging-in-Publication Data

Adare, Sierra.
    Mohawk / by Sierra Adare.
      p. cm. — (Native American peoples)
    Summary: A discussion of the history, culture, and contemporary life of the
Mohawk Indians.
    Includes bibliographical references and index.
    ISBN-10: 0-8368-3665-0   ISBN-13: 978-0-8368-3665-3 (lib. bdg.)
    1. Mohawk Indians—History—Juvenile literature. 2. Mohawk Indians—Social
life and customs—Juvenile literature. [1. Mohawk Indians.] I. Title. II. Series.
E99.M8A34   2003
974.7004'9755—dc21   2002191114

First published in 2003 by
Gareth Stevens Publishing
A Weekly Reader Company
1 Reader's Digest Rd.
Pleasantville, NY 10570-7000 USA

Produced by Discovery Books
Project editor: Valerie J. Weber
Designer and page production: Sabine Beaupré
Photo researcher: Rachel Tisdale
Native American consultant: D. L. Birchfield, J.D., Associate Professor of Native American
  Studies, University of Lethbridge, Alberta
Maps and diagrams: Stefan Chabluk
Gareth Stevens editorial direction: Mark Sachner
Gareth Stevens art direction: Tammy Gruenewald
Gareth Stevens production: Jessica L. Yanke

Photo credits: Native Stock: cover, pp. 4 (bottom), 7, 13, 14, 15 (both), 18, 23 (top), 25 (top);
North Wind Picture Archives: pp. 4 (top), 6, 9 (both), 10 (top); Peter Newark's American
Pictures: pp. 8, 10 (bottom), 19 (both); Corbis: pp. 11, 16, 21 (both), 23 (bottom), 24; Sierra
Adare: p. 26; Art Directors and Trip Photo Library: p. 20.

Printed in the United States of America

3 4 5 6 7 8 9 10 09 08

Cover: This Mohawk man carries a water drum, a traditional instrument among eastern North
American Indian people.

Contents

Words that appear in the glossary are printed in
boldface type the first time they appear in the text.

Origins

Land of the Mohawks

The Mohawk people live mostly in northern New York State and across the border in Canada; they number around twenty-five thousand. The Mohawks call themselves *Kanien'kehake*, which means "People of the Flint" because of the flint quarries in the eastern part of their territory. *Mohawk* means "cowards" in the language of the Abenaki Indians, traditional enemies and neighbors of the Mohawks. Although the Mohawks were considered powerful warriors, the Dutch and British traders soon used the Abenaki term Mohawk because it was easier to pronounce.

No one knows for sure how Mohawks and other Native Americans came to North America, but for centuries, most Native cultures have told stories about their origins. Long ago, according to a traditional Mohawk story, people lived in the Sky World. One day, a hole opened up at the base of a great tree. Sky Woman fell through it toward the sea, which completely covered Earth. A group of blue herons caught her. She then lived on the back of a great sea turtle floating on the water. There, she gave birth to a daughter, who had twin boys. Soon many people lived on Turtle Island, the Mohawks' name for Earth.

Though he probably never saw an Indian, an eighteenth-century artist drew this Mohawk man's clothing right. However, he added an incorrect bow and feather. Also, Mohawks never wore a bone in their nose.

The turtle (right) symbolizes Earth. On her back is the white pine Tree of Peace.

Mohawk elders also tell of the people coming from the American Southwest. According to this belief, thousands of years before history was written down, the Mohawks slowly moved into what is now the northeastern United States. Their homelands extended from modern central New York State up into Canada.

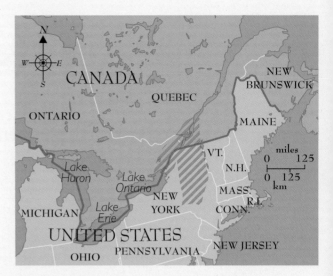

The Mohawks' original homelands stretched through today's New York State and areas of Quebec and Ontario.

Several scientific theories have been proposed to explain the origins of Native Americans, including the Mohawks. The most common theory is that thousands of years ago, people crossed a land mass between Asia and North America in the region now called the Bering Strait. Other scientists think Native Americans might have come to the Americas by sea. They would have then migrated across South, Central, and North America.

The Mohawk Language

Mohawk is an oral language. It was not written down until priests came to **convert** Mohawks to Christianity. The priests believed the Mohawks were not smart enough to understand more than twelve letters of the English alphabet so the Mohawk written language uses only twelve letters.

Mohawk	Pronunciation	English
sekoh	say-go	hello
yoh	yo	so long
hen'en	ha-a	yes
yah	e-yah	no
yeksa' ah	yek-saw	girl
raksa' ha	lock-saw	boy

History

Mohawks Form the Haudenosaunee Confederacy

The people in the Iroquoian language groups, which include the Mohawks, refer to themselves as Haudenosaunee, meaning "the people building a longhouse." This large wood and bark structure housed families of the same **clan**. The word "long-house" not only describes Haudenosaunee multifamily homes, but also the multination league the Mohawks founded.

A village was made up of several longhouses with a fence made of long stakes surrounding them.

A Message of Peace

Centuries before the arrival of the Europeans, Mohawks often fought against four other Haudenosaunee nations — the Oneida, Cayuga, Seneca, and Onondaga. Then came a man known as Skennenrahawi, or the Peacemaker, a man of great vision. He knew the only way the Haudenosaunee nations could stand up to their common enemy, the Algonquians, was to unite. He also knew the nations respected the brave Mohawk warriors. If the Mohawks agreed to peace, the others would too.

As the first to accept the Peacemaker's Great Law of Peace, the Mohawks are the "older brother" in the Haudenosaunee Confederacy. The Oneidas, Cayugas, and Senecas soon joined, but the Onondagas delayed until their leader was convinced of the wisdom of the Great Law. In 1722, a southeastern tribe, the Tuscaroras, joined, making it the Confederacy of Six Nations. The French called the Confederacy and its members the "Iroquois"; Mohawks prefer their own word, "Haudenosaunee."

Early Contact with Europeans

Living in villages between what is now Albany, New York, and Quebec in Canada, the Mohawk people were the farthest east of all the Haudenosaunee Confederacy. Thus, they were the first in the Confederacy to come into contact with the Europeans arriving

～ww～ Aiionwatha and Wampum Belts ～ww～

An Onondagan, Aiionwatha made the first **wampum belt** by stringing together purple and white shell beads. Their design represented the parts of the Great Law of Peace, a system of rules for behavior between individuals and groups. Aiionwatha used the belt to teach the Mohawks and other Haudenosaunees the Great Law. Called *Anakoha*, wampum belts are sacred to the Mohawks.

This wampum belt fragment recounts the historic forming of the Haudenosaunee Confederacy. The squares stand for four of the original five nations linked with the Tree of Peace.

in North America, meeting the French in 1534, the Dutch in 1609, and the English in 1664.

During the late 1500s, the Mohawks were at war with the Algonquians, who wanted to expand their territory. In exchange for furs, the French traded weapons to the Algonquians. Thus the Mohawks welcomed Dutch traders and the guns they supplied for the Native war. In 1613, the Mohawks and the Dutch formed an **alliance** and agreed to a **treaty**. This treaty, the first between Mohawks and Europeans, was called the Covenant Chain and was recorded on the Two-Row Wampum Belt. The rows ran next to each other the length of the belt. This pattern meant each nation would recognize and honor the other as an independent and equal nation. In 1664, the Dutch handed over control of the lands they had settled on in North America to the English, who renewed the Covenant Chain with the Mohawks.

Teoniahigarawe and the British

Mohawk leader Teoniahigarawe, called Hendricks by Europeans, met with British governor George Clinton in New York in 1753. Ignoring treaties, Clinton had broken the Covenant Chain by allowing more British settlers to move onto Mohawk land. When Clinton refused to honor the Covenant Chain and remove the settlers. Teoniahigarawe told him, "My heart aches because we Mohawks have always been faithful to you. . . . The covenant chain is broken."

Teoniahigarawe posed in European-style dress for this formal portrait by Dutch painter John Verelst while visiting Queen Anne in England in 1710.

Sir William Johnson, the trader and soldier who lived among the Mohawks, married a Mohawk woman whom the British called Molly Brant. Her Mohawk name is unknown.

The British Empire, preparing to wage war against France over territory in Europe and North America, sent Sir William Johnson to settle its differences with Teoniahigarawe. Johnson persuaded Teoniahigarawe to renew the Covenant Chain. The British did not, however, keep their part of the Covenant Chain agreement; settlers continued to take Mohawk land.

The Mohawks gave the British their first victory in what became known as the French and Indian War (1754–63) at the Battle of Lake George in 1755, where Teoniahigarawe died. With the help of the Mohawks and other Native nations, the British pushed the French out of much of North America.

Produced in 1771, this map shows the locations of the independent nations of the Haudenosaunees in what is currently New York State and Canada.

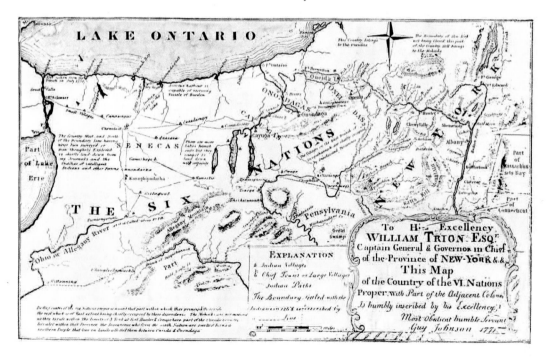

Thayendanegea, also known as Joseph Brant, fought for the British during the American Revolution and acted as translator between the British and the Mohawks.

Mohawks in the American Revolution

The American Revolution divided the Haudenosaunee Confederacy into those who fought for the British and those who fought for the Americans. Sir Johnson's Mohawk brother-in-law, Joseph Brant, persuaded four of the nations to side with the British, including the Mohawks.

In 1778, Brant's forces defeated American troops. Wanting to crush the Native forces, General George Washington ordered that all Haudenosaunees, including those allied with the Americans, should not "merely be overrun but destroyed." Within a year, Mohawk territory in today's New York State was destroyed, laid to waste by General John Sullivan's "scorched-earth" policy. His troops burned villages, corn fields, fruit orchards — everything — to the ground. They killed every man, woman, and child they could find. More starved to death that winter.

U.S. General John Sullivan led soldiers in a number of battles against both the British and Native Americans, during the American Revolution.

The 1783 Treaty of Paris signed by the Americans and British ended the American Revolution. It also set up the U.S.-Canadian border through Mohawk country.

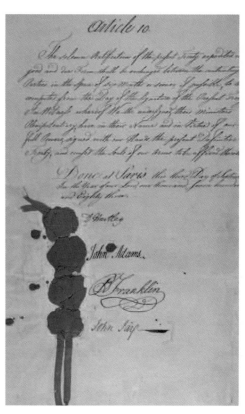

In Canada and the United States

At the end of the Revolution in 1783 when the colonies became the United States, many Mohawks followed Brant into British-held Canada. The government gave 1,200 square miles (3,100 square kilometers) of land on the Grand River in Ontario to Brant in 1784 to "take possession of and . . . enjoy forever." As members of all Haudenosaunee nations fled the United States, Grand River became the center of the Canadian side of the Haudenosaunee Confederacy. There have been two separate Confederacies ever since.

Mohawks who remained in their Mohawk Valley homeland signed a treaty with the United States at Fort Stanwix in 1784 that clearly defined the boundaries of the Mohawks' land. Mohawks never surrendered their homelands and did not give up their right to define themselves as a separate nation or to run their own lives with their own traditional form of government.

Mohawks Forced to Move

After the American Revolution, most Mohawks were forced to resettle around Akwesasne — today a reservation in northern New York State and Ontario and Quebec, Canada — or in other

The Indians live much better than most of the Mohawk River farmers, their Houses very well furnished with all necessary Household utensils, great plenty of Grain, several Horses, cows and waggons (sic). . . . The town . . . consisted of [128] houses, mostly very large and elegant.

U.S. General John Sullivan's officers and men praising the wealth of the Mohawk towns they were destroying

locations in Canada. The 1783 Treaty of Paris set the boundary between Canada and the United States, drawing it right through Mohawk territory.

The War of 1812 continued the fight between the British and the Americans. As in the American Revolution, the British wanted Mohawks to fight as their ally. However, the Mohawks remained neutral until the American and British forces fought a battle on Mohawk lands at Akwesasne. Defending their lands forced the Mohawks into the war, again splitting the people between those who fought for the Americans and those who fought for the British.

During the mid-1800s, New York State unsuccessfully tried to get the U.S. government to move the Mohawks to Indian Territory (present-day Oklahoma) west of the Mississippi River. The Canadians, however, did succeed in seizing Mohawk land along the Grand River in Canada and refused to return it to the Mohawks. Eventually, both the Canadian and U.S. governments passed laws that forced Mohawks off their traditional lands and onto reservations.

Children Taken from Their Families

On both sides of the United States-Canadian border, whites stole Mohawk children from the reservations and sent them far away to boarding schools. At these schools, children were not allowed to speak the Mohawk language, wear their own clothes, or follow their own religion. They were mistreated and many died. Others ran away.

The Twentieth Century

During the early and mid-1900s, the U.S. and Canadian governments continued their policies from the 1700s. They denied the Mohawks their right as an independent nation to practice their traditional government, religious beliefs, and customs. The governments also refused to allow Mohawk women the right to vote in tribal affairs.

This modern Mohawk man wears the traditional clothing of his people, celebrating — and helping to educate others about — his culture.

The Mohawks, however, continued to practice their traditions in secret.

By the late 1900s, Mohawks and other Haudenosaunees began to openly practice their traditional form of government, religious beliefs, and customs despite objections from the U.S. and Canadian governments. Mohawk women now publicly help form the traditional government, participate in religious ceremonies, and teach Mohawk customs, history, and beliefs to children. Today, members of the Haudenosaunee (Iroquois) nations have their own passports and have appeared before the United Nations representing independent nations, despite the objections of the U.S. and Canadian governments.

Democracy in Action?

In 1885, the Canadian government forced its own version of tribal leadership on the Mohawks. First, it declared the traditional Mohawk government to be illegal and put the traditionally elected Mohawk leaders of Akwesasne in prison. The Canadians then picked fifteen other Mohawks, got them drunk, and then forced them to choose as leaders Akwesasne residents whom the Canadian government believed would do whatever it told them to do. As one Akwesasne sachem, or leader, Michael Mitchell described the Canadians' conduct in 1989, "This is the way Canada introduced our people to the principles of their democracy."

Traditional Way of Life

Longhouses were windproof, and their roofs resisted rain, ice, and snow. Shelves for storage lined the interior.

Mohawk Home Life

Traditionally, Mohawks lived in villages consisting of several longhouses made of elm bark covering poles bent in an upside-down U shape. The longhouses were usually 20 feet (6 meters) wide and 150 feet (46 m) long. Several families lived in a single longhouse.

Mohawks are matrilineal, which means that all children belong to their mother's clan. They are also matrilocal, which means that after marriage men move to the wife's home. Women control the land, deciding what to plant and where. Traditionally, Mohawk women raised corn, melons, squash, pumpkin, beans, tobacco, sunflowers, and peas. They kept apple orchards and tapped maple trees for syrup and sugar. Girls learned gardening from their mothers and aunts.

Mohawk men traveled throughout their territory, hunting, fishing, and trading with other Native nations. Boys learned from their fathers and uncles how to fish, hunt, and clear the land.

Before contact with Europeans, Mohawks dressed in two-piece deerskin garments, leggings, and moccasins embroidered with porcupine quills. Men wore feather head-dresses for ceremonies. Later **broadcloth** clothing replaced deerskin, and trade beads replaced quills. Women wore **pantalets**, overdresses of calico, and blankets like shawls. They also carried beaded pocketbooks.

The beadwork on these Mohawk moccasins is done in a traditional design using modern beads. The original trade beads were darker.

Tewaarathon: A Spiritual Practice

In traditional Mohawk culture, playing the game of *Tewaarathon,* is a way of thanking the Creator, who gave the game to the Mohawks, for the gifts of life to all things on Mother Earth. During the late eighteenth century, whites, who believed it was a war game, discouraged the Mohawks from playing Tewaarathon. But, in fact, Mohawks have never stopped playing the game.

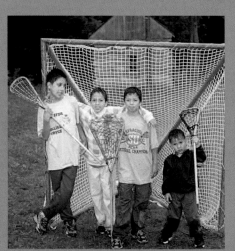

The size of the field depends on the number of players. Traditionally, two teams, each numbering from five to one thousand people, played on a field that could be between 100 yards (91 m) and 2 miles (3 km) long. Historically and in modern times, players throw or carry a ball to their goal at the far end of the field using sticks with nets.

Named *lacrosse* by non-Natives, Tewaarathon is played by children and adults of all ages.

Both the Thanksgiving Address and the Code of Handsome Lake stress the Mohawks' sense of responsibility for taking good care of the land and all its beauties.

Beliefs

At the core of Mohawk belief is the Creator, who shares power with others — trees, plants, animals, water, other spirits, and people — who are often messengers for the Creator. The Mohawks give thanks to the Creator and all living things through the Thanksgiving Address, which dates back to the origins of the Haudenosaunees and is not related to U.S. or Canadian Thanksgiving holidays. According to tradition, Sky Woman's son, the Good Minded Twin, began this method of offering thanks for all of creation. The Address has always been and continues to be spoken at the beginning and closing of all ceremonies and governmental meetings.

The Address has fifteen or sixteen sections and reminds all Haudenosaunees how they are connected to everything in the universe. Each section starts by naming the things Creator has provided, such as the earth, animals, birds, and bodies of water, and describing their purpose, duties, and responsibilities and how they are connected with all living things. For example, the Creator created many varieties of meadow grasses that grow every spring and bring pleasure to all people, including children. Grasses also bring happiness to the animals that eat the grasses and the birds that use the grasses to build their nests. People are reminded throughout every section to be grateful and offer thanks. All sections end with "So it will be in our minds."

In 1799, a Seneca man named Skaniateriio (or Handsome Lake) received visions from the Creator in the form of four messengers. The messengers brought Handsome Lake a new code for living for the Haudenosaunee people. The code contained 130 messages, stories, songs, ceremonies, and addresses to be used with the Thanksgiving Address. This code, called the *Gaiwiio,* or the "Great Good Message," stresses the importance of maintaining strong traditional families, honoring tribal ways, and caring for the land. Besides upholding old ways, the code provided help in adjusting to the changes forced on the Haudenosaunees after the American Revolution.

Commonly called the Longhouse Religion, the Code of Handsome Lake is currently practiced by many Mohawks. Every autumn, people go to their local community's longhouse, on or off the reservation, for three days to hear the Code.

∿∿∿ The Code of Handsome Lake ∿∿∿

The Code tells the people how to continue ceremonies that renew both individuals and the community. It teaches how and why to give thanksgiving when planting food, how to care for the land, and how to adjust to living on the smaller plots on reservations. The Code discourages drinking and gambling and advises Mohawk parents on how to raise a family who will help the community. It also recounts Handsome Lake's journey to the Creator's land and teaches historical events.

Traditional Government

The Mohawk Nation has three clans — Turtle, Wolf, and Bear. Traditionally, the oldest woman becomes the Clan Mother, the head of the clan. The Clan Mother selects the leader, the peacekeeper, and the **faithkeeper** for her clan. These men are called sachems rather than chiefs. Once the clan approves the Clan Mother's choices, the sachems form the leadership of the Mohawk Nation.

These leaders, or sachems, also become part of the *rotiiane*, the Grand Council of the Haudenosaunee Confederacy, made up of fifty leaders from the Six Nations. These leaders serve for life unless they are "dehorned" (removed from office) by the Clan Mothers.

This basket in the shape of a turtle represents one of the Mohawk clans as well as Turtle Island, as Earth was known in the Mohawk origin story.

How Clan Mothers Choose Leaders

Clan Mothers watch male children from birth through manhood to determine who will make good leaders. They select men for leadership positions based on four rules: A man must be married with at least one child. He must have committed no crime. He must not have expressed a desire to become a leader. He must not have shown any improper behavior, especially toward women.

Honeeyeathtawnorow, from the Wolf clan, met with Queen Anne. He is shown here in European-style clothing. The dog at his feet is Dutch artist John Verelst's idea of what a North American wolf looked like.

Sagayeathquapiethtow, member of the Bear clan, was a Mohawk leader who also met with Queen Anne. He wears a European-style toga and cape. The London *Daily Courant* newspaper stated that his tattoos were more impressive than scary.

The Grand Council passes all laws for the Six Nations. All fifty leaders must agree on every law, a concept called governing by **consensus**. The Haudenosaunees call this kind of governing "one heart, one mind, one head, and one body" for the peace and power of the Six Nations. Unfortunately, historically and in more recent years, both the U.S. and Canadian governments have tried to force the Mohawks to give up their traditional form of government.

The Great Law of Peace still guides all traditional members of the Haudenosaunee Confederacy as they go about their daily lives. Passed down from grandparents to grandchildren, this guideline tells each person how to behave toward others. The basic principles of the Great Law of Peace are good behavior toward each other, good behavior within the Confederacy, positive spiritual beliefs, and a positive attitude toward all other forms of life.

Reservation Life

Almost from their arrival, Europeans forced Mohawks to **assimilate** to white culture by wearing European-style clothing and practicing European customs, laws, languages, and religion. Children who went to church-run schools at Akwesasne and on other reservations were punished for speaking Mohawk or practicing the Longhouse religion. They were also discouraged from playing Tewaarathon (lacrosse). Mohawk children were taught only Euro-American history and languages.

Today Mohawk children are learning their language again. This sign — "Our children's future, everyone's responsibility" — appears on the Kahnawake Indian Reserve, a Mohawk reservation near Montreal in Canada.

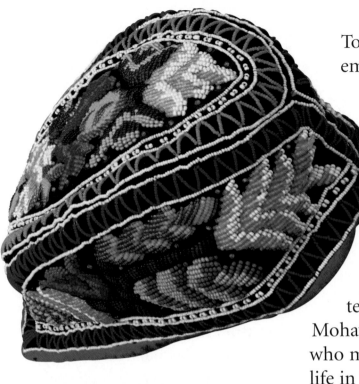

Today, reservation life emphasizes more Mohawk traditions and values. During the late 1900s, Mohawk Ray Fadden-Tenahetorens, became the first teacher at Akwesasne to teach true Mohawk history at the reservation school. He refused to use standard textbooks that showed Mohawks as stupid savages who made no contributions to life in North America. When he retired, he built the Six Nations Museum in Onchiota, New York.

This Mohawk hat beaded with a floral design and Haudenosaunee vessel from around 1500 are both displayed at the Six Nations Museum.

Mohawk Views of Reservations

If only we were left alone, we could redevelop our society . . . which was old in **democracy** when Europe knew only **monarchs**.
Ernest Benedict (Mohawk), 1941

No nation has the right to hold a captive nation.
Mohawk Warrior Society, 1981

Today

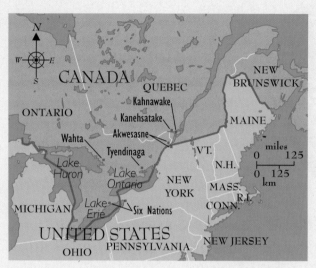

Varying in size, Mohawk reservations are scattered along the eastern border of the United States and Canada.

The Contemporary Mohawks

Today, over 25,000 Mohawks live on and off reservations all over the United States and Canada, 80 percent of them within Canada, where there are three reservations — Kahnawake, Kanesatake, and Akwesasne, which straddles the U.S.-Canadian border. Akwesasne, the only reservation in the United States, is the biggest, with a total of 22,230 acres (9,000 ha). As of 2002, about 13,400 Mohawks lived in Akwesasne, about 5,600 on the U.S. side and nearly 7,800 on the Canadian side. Nearly 8,000 Mohawks live at Kahnawake (near Montreal), which is 12,500 acres (5,060 ha), while Kanesatake (near Oka, Quebec) has about 1,800 Mohawks living on 2,370 acres (960 ha).

Akwesasne has three internal Mohawk governments: The United States forced one government on the Mohawks (the St. Regis Tribal Council); Canada forced a second one (the Mohawk Council of Akwesasne); and the Mohawks chose their own traditional government. Struggles for power between the two federal governmental systems have created problems for the Mohawks.

For example, in Akwesasne, the St. Regis Tribal Council has allowed the opening of **casinos**, which the traditional government opposes. Many Mohawks live by the Great Law of Peace and do not accept casinos, seeing them as bad for both individuals and the community. Others see the casinos as a source of jobs and income in an area that needs both.

Many Mohawks own gas stations, tobacco shops, or small businesses producing craft items. Others have also left the reservations seeking work.

Today, some Mohawks make their living by producing **sweetgrass** and wooden baskets such as these, Native beadwork, or handmade snowshoes.

Whether they live on or off the reservation, Mohawks today drive cars, go to school, work in offices, in factories, or on farms, attend universities, and speak English or French. They also participate in Longhouse religious ceremonies, play Tewaarathon for traditional reasons, and speak Mohawk.

Mohawk Sky Walkers

The original "sky walkers," Mohawk high-steel construction workers in New York City.

One Mohawk occupation dates back to the 1880s, when Americans built a bridge across the St. Lawrence River on Mohawk land. As white men worked high up on the narrow beams, Mohawk men and youths would follow them up the beams to watch as they riveted the bridge together. Men willing to work many hundreds of feet above the ground were rare, so bridge engineers taught the Mohawks to work in high-steel construction.

By the 1920s, Mohawks were routinely braving heights. In 1955, Mohawks placed a 222-foot (68-m) television tower on top of the 1,470-foot (450-m) Empire State Building in New York City.

Authors, Artists, and Actors

Many Mohawk children have grown up to become successful authors, artists, and actors. Doug George-Kanentiio grew up on the Akwesasne Reservation. Since his school days, he has written about important Mohawk issues for newspapers. He edited *Akwesasne Notes* news journal for six years. He also **negotiated** for the Mohawk Nation to get the U.S. government to live up to its treaty agreements.

Artist Bill Powless draws cartoons for the Six Nations (Haudenosaunee) Reserve newspaper *Tekawennake* in Ontario, Canada. He uses a character that acts like Tonto, a character in the 1950s *Lone Ranger* television series, to address local issues from both serious and funny viewpoints.

Although portrayed as little more than a **sidekick** and servant to the Lone Ranger, Tonto is a popular figure on Mohawk reservations. The actor who played Tonto on TV and in movies was Mohawk Jay Silverheels, who grew up on the Six Nations Reserve.

Mohawk actor Jay Silverheels *(right)* founded the Indian Actors Workshop in Hollywood to help more Natives find roles and change the movie image of Indians.

The Sweetgrass Singers, a group of Mohawk women, perform in traditional dress.

Photographer Shelley Niro also uses Hollywood images to poke fun at the "Indian princess" image. In her photograph *Final Frontier, First Frame, 1992,* she dressed like a member of TV's *Star Trek* crew. She learned the art of photography by taking photos of her mother and sisters in the attic of the family's home. Niro wanted to show the strength of Mohawk women, Mohawk pride in being Native, and the fact that Mohawks could have fun, too.

The Smoke Dance

When the wind shifted and longhouses became smoky, elders would ask the young people to dance the smoke away. Drummers played a fast beat on water drums, while dancers spun and twisted. The movement forced the smoke to rise and escape through the vent in the roof. The best dancers stopped the instant the drum hit its final beat.

This is the origin of the traditional Smoke Dance. Today, Smoke Dancers dressed in traditional Haudenosaunee outfits perform at powwows. Judges watch for dancers staying with the drumbeat and stopping on time with the end of the song.

Reclaiming the Land

The 1784 Six Nations treaty guaranteed the original five nations of the Haudenosaunee Confederacy their right to their land in New York State. Claiming the state has refused to keep that treaty agreement, five nations of the original Haudenosaunee Confederacy have taken New York State to court over what has been called land-claims issues. In 1989, the Mohawks asked the judge to force the state to give the Mohawks some **public lands**. They've also asked the state to pay rent for land taken from the Mohawks and for the right to buy land offered for sale to add to their small reservation.

Kanatsiohareke, "the place of the clean pot," is a traditional community in the heart of the Mohawk Valley, the traditional land of the Mohawks.

Tom Porter and Kanatsiohareke

In 1993, a group of Mohawks headed by elder Tom Porter purchased a 377-acre (153-ha) farm in the Mohawk Valley. There they have reestablished a traditional community on land called Kanatsiohareke. Five to ten families live on the farm at any given time. They grow traditional foods, speak Mohawk, and observe traditional ceremonies.

At Kanatsiohareke, community members use both traditional ways and modern technology to live in harmony with the land; for example, they farm with horses as well as with a tractor. A spring supplies the farm's water and runs the **hydroelectric power** generator. In addition to making traditional crafts, they run a T-shirt shop and a bed-and-breakfast.

"To live in harmony with the Creator, we must live in harmony with nature," explains Porter. "We farm like my grandpa farmed and the generations who came before him."

Although the courts have still not made a final ruling on the Mohawks' lawsuit, some Mohawks are not waiting for the justice system to resolve land-claims issues. They are looking at projects such as Kanatsiohareke, the Mohawk community thriving on land purchased in the Mohawk Valley that had originally been part of the tribe's territory. This community has become a symbol of what Mohawks can achieve through living traditionally.

As for the survival of the Mohawks and the Haudenosaunee Confederacy, traditional Onondaga Sachem Oren Lyons sums it up best: "We will determine what our culture is. . . . We are not going to be put in a museum or accept your **interpretation** of our culture. . . .We will continue our ceremonies. We have the right to exist and that right does not come from you or your government."

Time Line

Centuries before Europeans	Skennenrahawi (the Peacemaker) brings the Great Law of Peace to the Mohawks, the first nation in the Haudenosaunee Confederacy.
1609	The Dutch make first contact with the Mohawks.
1613	Mohawks and the Dutch sign the first treaty between the Mohawks and Europeans, called the Covenant Chain.
1653	The Mohawks, along with the other nations in the Haudenosaunee Confederacy, make peace with the French.
1664	Mohawks transfer their alliance from the Dutch to the English, renewing the Covenant Chain.
1753	Teoniahigarawe (Hendricks) meets with Governor George Clinton in New York; the Covenant Chain is broken.
1755	The Battle of Lake George; Teoniahigarawe is killed.
1779	General John Sullivan destroys Mohawk villages.
1783	Treaty of Paris signed between the United States and Great Britain sets the boundary line between Canada and the United States through the middle of Mohawk territory.
1799	Skaniateriio (Handsome Lake) receives the Great Good Message and begins the Longhouse religion.
1812	U.S. and British forces fight a battle on Mohawk lands .
1867	Canada illegally seizes Mohawks' land on the Grand River.
1892	New York State creates the St. Regis Tribal Council and gives this council the right to rule over U.S. Mohawks.
1984	Gambling for profit begins on the Akwesasne Reservation.
1989	Mohawks submit a proposal to U.S. and New York State authorities for the return of lands illegally taken.
1993	Tom Porter heads a group of Mohawks who purchase land to reestablish a traditional community.
1999	New York moves to have the Mohawks' land claims dismissed.

Glossary

alliance: an agreement between two groups to work together on a common goal.

assimilate: to force one group to adopt the culture — the language, lifestyle, and values — of another.

broadcloth: a thick cloth woven from wool.

casinos: buildings that have slot machines, card games, and other gambling games.

clan: a group of related families.

consensus: agreement to an opinion or position by all individuals in a group.

convert: to cause a person to change a belief, usually a religious one.

democracy: government that is run by the people of a country or their elected representatives, not by a king, queen, or dictator.

faithkeeper: a tribal member who provides counsel and guidance for the leader.

hydroelectric power: electricity generated by moving water.

interpretation: how someone explains something or someone.

monarch: a king, queen, or other ruler of a state or country.

negotiate: to work with others to come to an agreement.

pantalets: long underpants.

public lands: land owned by the state that no one lives on, such as state forest land.

sidekick: a close companion or friend.

sweetgrass: a grass used widely by the Mohawks and other Native peoples for making crafts and for spiritual and trading purposes.

treaty: an agreement among nations.

wampum belt: differently colored beads made from shells strung into a belt in unique designs, which serve as reminders of historical events, laws, and treaties

More Resources

Web Sites:

http://sixnations.org For information on Mohawk history, culture, and traditional government.

http://www.tuscaroras.com/graydeer/pages/childrenspage.htm Activities for kids that focus on historic and contemporary information about the Mohawks.

http://www.rom.on.ca/digs/longhouse Information on Haudenosaunee longhouses.

Videos:

The Broken Chain. TNT Network, 1993.

The Iroquois Great Law of Peace. Kanatsiohareke Mohawk Community, [no date].

They Lied to You in School: Ray Fadden Speaks. White Buffalo Multi-Media Archives, [no date].

Books:

Bruchac, Joseph. *Children of the Longhouse.* Puffin, 1998.

Bruchac, Joseph. *Native American Stories.* Fulcrum, 1991.

Shenandoah, Joanne, and Douglas M. George. *Sky Woman: Legends of the Iroquois.* Clear Light Publishers, 1998.

Tehanetoens. *Legends of the Iroquois.* Book Publishing Co., 1998.

Tehanetoens. *Sacred Song of the Hermit Thrush: A Native American Legend.* Book Publishing Co., 1993.

Things to Think About and Do

Consensus Versus Majority Rules
In an example of true government by consensus, all fifty leaders of the Grand Council must agree on each law passed. Ask your teacher to explain how this is different from the U.S. idea of democracy and what the difference is between government by consensus and government by majority rule.

How to Pick a Leader
Clan Mothers follow four basic rules when selecting sachems. (See Chapter Three.) What do you think are the reasons for these rules? Why is a man who has a wife and family a better choice than a single man with no children? Explain your opinions in a paragraph or two.

Traditional Clothing
Go to http://www.tuscaroras.com/graydeer/pages/paperdolls.htm and download the paper doll for a traditionally dressed Haudenosuanee man and woman. Carefully cut out the paper dolls and their clothing. Using crayons or colored pencils, color their clothing as described on this web page, which is about traditional Haudenosuanee clothing.

Index